Frederick H. Seymour

A Canoe Trip; or, a Lark on the Water

Frederick H. Seymour

A Canoe Trip; or, a Lark on the Water

ISBN/EAN: 9783337144906

Printed in Europe, USA, Canada, Australia, Japan

Cover: Foto ©Andreas Hilbeck / pixelio.de

More available books at **www.hansebooks.com**

PRICE, 30 CENTS.

THE "ULYSSES."

A CANOE TRIP;

OR,

LARK ON THE WATER.

CRUISE OF THE "ULYSSES" FROM LAKE HURON
TO LAKE ERIE.

BY FREDERICK H. SEYMOUR.

ILLUSTRATIONS FROM SKETCHES BY THE AUTHOR.

> "A wet sheet and a flowing sea,
> A wind that follows fast,
> And fills the white and rustling sail,
> And bends the gallant mast."
> —COWPER.

PUBLISHED BY
THE DETROIT FREE PRESS COMPANY.
1880.

COPYRIGHT,
BY F. H. SEYMOUR,
1880.

PREFACE.

The chapters forming this little volume originally appeared as sketches in the *Detroit Free Press*. Encouraged by the growing interest in canoeing, and the conviction that as a manly, dignified and healthful recreation it is bound to attain a permanent popularity, as well as by letters from many persons interested in the subject, the writer has been induced to revise the sketches and offer them in book form.

F. H. S.

DETROIT, *November 1880.*

CHAPTER I.

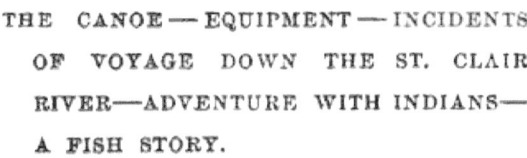

" 'Tis ever common
That men are merriest when they are from home."
—*Shakspeare.*

THE CANOE — EQUIPMENT — INCIDENTS OF VOYAGE DOWN THE ST. CLAIR RIVER—ADVENTURE WITH INDIANS—A FISH STORY.

ECIDEDLY the "canoe fever" is insidious. Ever since reading McGregor's exploits in the canoe, "Rob Roy," a small boat capable of being carried in an emergency—arranged to be slept in and easily propelled—in which extensive journeys had been made throughout Europe and the East, I have been possessed with the idea of making a trip in a "cruising canoe."

Canoeing has become quite the thing in England and is rapidly becoming popular in this country, so much so that the principal cities now boast their "canoe clubs." I bought a Racine veneer canoe, weight sixty pounds, with its equipments, viz., a double-bladed paddle, jointed; a mast, also jointed; a sail, combined life preserver, cushion and mattress, and without formality it was dubbed "Ulysses," after

> "That sagacious man
> Who, having overthrown the sacred town
> Of Ilium, wandered far, and visited
> The capitals of many nations, learned
> The customs of their dwellers, and endured
> Great suffering on the deep."

It contained apparatus for steering with the feet, and water and air-tight compartments in which to stow the outfit. Although it is claimed that oars are more effective, the beauty of the paddle as a means of locomotion is that the navigator faces the way he is going, and paddling is far less of an exertion than rowing. Twenty miles a day can be accomplished without much fatigue, even by a person unaccustomed to the exercise, and then the little sail, with a favoring wind, will send the canoe along at a fast rate, while the happy voyager leans back on his cushion and sees the varied panorama on shore pass him by.

Joe, like "Barkis," was "willin'," so we planned a week's cruise. We decided to make a trip from Lake Huron to Lake Erie. Down the St. Clair river, which separates the

United States from Canada, to the famous marshes or "Flats" at the mouth of the river, in Lake St. Clair; down one of the numerous channels through "the Flats," to the Canada shore of the lake and around the shore to Detroit, near the entrance of the Detroit river, at the extreme foot of Lake St. Clair, and from thence southward to Lake Erie. The dotted lines upon the map indicate the route taken. We prepared ourselves with the following outfit, which is given for the benefit of any one contemplating such a cruise:

CLOTHING.

Slippers (to wear in the canoe).
Stout shoes.
Two pair socks.
Two pair pants (one pair on, of course).
One heavy coat.
Two flannel undershirts.
One blue overshirt.
Two pair drawers.
One rubber blanket.
Two pair woolen blankets.
One air pillow.

We also took an alcohol stove, compass, liquor (only to be used in emergency), twine and cord, sketching materials, opera glass, revolver, charts, etc., etc.

PROVISIONS.

Liebig's extract of beef.
Pressed beef.
Condensed milk.
Coffee and sugar.
Lemons.
Canned soups.
Sardines, salmon, etc., etc.
Cooking utensils.

I devised a small tent to spread over the canoe at night, supported by the mast and boom and capable of being rolled into small compass. The whole outfit, including tent, weighing less than ninety pounds, was stowed away in handy packages in the water-tight compartments of the canoe.

We took a steamer from Detroit to Lake Huron. Joe was so very solicitous about having his canoe placed near the gangway, that when on being accused of preparing to get rich by charging the passengers ten dollars a head for saving them in case anything happened to the steamboat, he only blushed and answered not a word.

It was at 9 o'clock one beautiful morning that we launched our canoes, the "*Halloo*" and "*Ulysses*," off the dock at Port Huron, amid a shower of comments from a large crowd which never failed us at every other place, civilized or otherwise, thereafter that we departed from.

As we paddled out along the dock a thick-set man with a crooked nose followed and saluted me thus:

"I say!"

I knew he did, but I did not trouble myself to tell him so, and he continued:

"Look-a-here!"

But I wouldn't and he began to get mad.

A RACE.

"Hello! I s-a-a-a-y!" he yelled again. I knew he said it; he needn't have told me he said it; I could have heard him a mile, and I would have taken his word for it any way. There are people who get mad at you for minding your own business.

"Look-a-here!" my gentle friend continued, "you blank, smash, dashed, something or other!" and as he communed with himself after this truly enthusiastic manner, and finally commenced to paw around on the dock for something to throw, I threw up the little sail and with a favorable wind skimmed down the river aided by a current of six miles an hour, Joe following close behind.

The breeze freshened and everything indicated that we would make the mouth of the river by night. We met numbers of vessels coming up the river, and the passengers on one large Lake Superior propeller crowded to the rail and railed at us as we shot past. At one point we ran in close to the bank of the river on the American side; a man driving a horse and buggy came into view on the highway, which ran for quite a distance beside the shore. We challenged him; he whipped up his horse and we had a merry race for nearly a mile, when the road wound out of view.

Marine City was reached at one o'clock, where we

dined. Here an old lady, with tears in her eyes, sought our acquaintance, and having learned of our proposed journey, requested that we keep a lookout for the body of her little grandson, supposed to have been drowned in the St. Clair river

At three o'clock we made the head of Walpole Island, on the Dominion side, and landed to consult the charts, in order to decide our future course. We encountered an old Indian. He was seated alone on the shore, and responded to our salutations with a feeble grin and the faintest—very faintest—suspicion of a wink in the northeast corner of his left eye.

Joe poised himself in front of the noble red man, and, in the language of Shakspeare, held forth to him thus:

> "Tell me, sweet Lord, what is't that takes from thee
> Thy stomach, pleasure, and thy golden sleep?
> Why dost thou bend thine eyes upon the earth,
> And sit around like a Stoughton bottle
> Or an inanimate tobacco sign?
> Why hast thou lost the fresh bloom in thy cheeks,
> Hast thy girl gone back on thee,
> Or worse, dost thy mother-in-law visit thee,
> And raise cantankerous ruction 'round thy wigwam door?"

This extraordinary burst of eloquence was rewarded with as many as ten grunts and a snort. The Indian

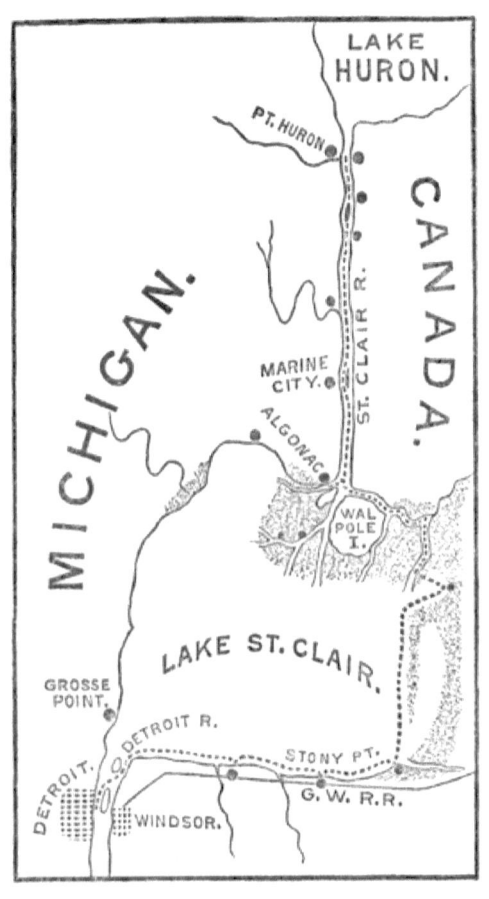

MAP OF ROUTE FROM LAKE HURON TO DETROIT.

could not speak English. He then left, and brought another Indian, who, I suppose, was noted for his English education. He informed us that the island was "Injun reserve," and that the old man was "boss," "Him chief." At this juncture several more Indians approached, and, after refusing their demand for "fire water," and treating them to tobacco, we hoisted sail for Algonac, a small village nearly opposite, in Michigan. We landed amid the piercing observations of a crowd of about one hundred spectators. After a vain attempt to get a deaf man to watch our canoes, we started to procure some provisions. Aside from looking like brigands, perhaps, we knew of no reason why our advent should create so profound a sensation.

I had omitted to get my liquor flask filled, so we went to the combined dry goods, grocery, crockery, drug and hardware store, also post office.

I asked the young man for whisky.

"Can't let you have it," said he.

"Why?"

"You must have a physician's prescription," he replied.

"Well, I can give you one," said I boldly.

"Are you a doctor?"

"I am!" and I here thought of G. W.'s little hatchet.

18 AN EMBARRASSING SITUATION.

"Here's a blank," producing one, "fill it out properly for what you want."

I cogitated for a moment or two, and here is what I produced:

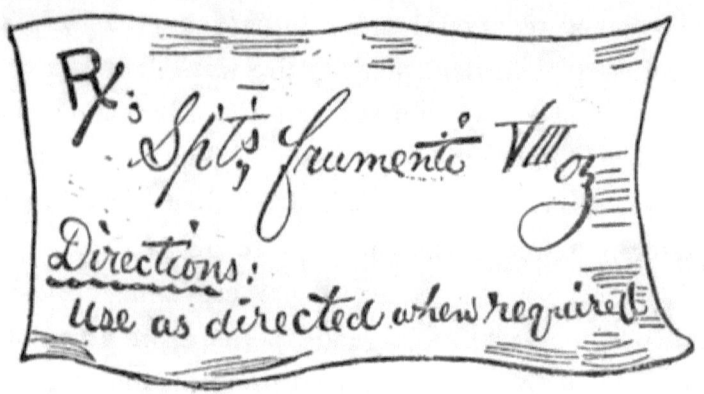

The young man gave a bewildered look at my sunburnt nose, and went to put it up. We went out to make other purchases, and on our return found the entire store occupied by a bevy of young ladies; the young man behind the counter, with a worried look on his classic features, was busy distributing the mail, and every blessed pair of eyes in every blessed one of those blessed heads was fixed upon us two bashful young men when we came in. We had to wait for the young man. Our situation was truly embarrassing. Had we been dressed in the usual attire of civilized travelers we would have been flattered, but to

AN ALGONAC HORSE BLOCK.

be caught with red Turkish fezes on our heads, with blue shirts and knee breeches on, and with long stockings, by a score or more of pretty girls, was too, too much. How they did stare at us. Joe hid one of his shins behind a rake handle, and I retreated to the friendly shelter of a sausage-stuffer. Finally the young man came up smiling, and said, so loudly that every one of the damsels heard him:

"Oh! you have come for that whisky!" and handed us a big black bottle that would hold nearly a gallon.

We fled from the store amid a chorus of laughter. Joe and I are going up there to assassinate that young man.

When we reached our canoes we found a regular mass meeting assembled — the whole male population. Joe asked a slim man "if any one was sick in Algonac?" The slim man said "Yes." Joe gave an agonized look upward, heaved a mighty sigh, and responded: "Then they are not *all* here."

It was destined that I was to make the rest of the trip alone. Joe received here a message compelling him to return to Detroit that night by the steamer; so bidding him farewell I paddled around to the head of Russel's Island, a small islet near Walpole, and selecting a smooth piece of grass, hauled the boat up, spread the little tent, looked after my kitchen, and before the sun sank had supper cooked and eaten. I had intended to camp on Walpole Island, but when we were having our interview with the Indians, Joe observed them making comments on the revolver, opera glasses, tackle, and other things in my canoe, and advised me not to encamp there.

Very soon darkness came on and the moon rose. I entered the canoe under the little tent, lit the lantern and read awhile. Before retiring for the night I observed that the light inside made the tent very conspicuous. Dismissing the idea of Indian raids, I turned in and was soon asleep. About eleven o'clock I was awakened by the low murmur of voices and the chance striking of a paddle against the side of a "dug-out." Grasping my revolver, I sprang up and stepped out of the tent. The bright moonlight made visible, just entering a fringe of reeds lining the shore, a canoe propelled by two Indians, who, immediately on seeing me, turned and paddled for Walpole Island with many guttural exclamations. An unpleasant interruption, but I was tired, turned in again and was soon asleep. However, I slept lightly, and at two o'clock another unwonted sound awakened me in an instant. I was on an uninhabited island alone. I might be robbed and murdered and no one would be the wiser. These reflections flashed through my mind as the sound of the paddle and the murmured voices coming nearer and nearer was again heard. I laid still until they ceased, awaiting developments. I cut a slit through the tent to see what was going on, to no purpose; but was startled into action by hearing a whisper. They had landed above me, out of sight. I gently unfastened the tent curtain, threw it open and peeped out. There were my friends on shore and coming toward me; but my action had arrested attention, and one of them said, in very good English: "John! that fellow sees us!" They straightway ran to their canoe, embarked hastily, and made the water eddy behind their paddle as they directed their course across the river.

I came out of the tent, and I felt half tempted to empty my revolver after them, as I watched the marauders in the moonlight paddle across the channel, and disappear in the shadow of the island.

It was cold and damp outside, and, going back to the canoe for warmth, before I realized it, was asleep, nor did I awake until the morning sun illuminated the tent. My scalp was on, my throat uncut, and nothing but the slit in the tent remained to show that the night's experience was not a dream. Throwing off the blankets, and sticking my nose out into the sunshine, I gazed on my little island domain, and felt as independent as—well, as a modern servant maid.

Breakfast prepared and dispatched, and outfit stowed in the canoe, I paddled to the head of the little island and stopped to sketch an old wreck. While doing this a huge, long-legged bird alighted near at hand, cocked his head to one side, and struck an attitude in which grandeur was elegantly blended with studied ease. His attitude was so arrogant that it awakened hostility, and I fired the revolver at him, which did not seem to disturb his majestic contemplations in the least. Landing with the paddle, and on going toward him to see if he was stuffed, he "lit—out."

The course planned for the day's cruise was through the "Chenel Ecarte," meaning clear water, an old French name, Anglicised by the sailors into the "Sni Carty Channel." It circles around the head of Walpole Island and runs in a tortuous course through the marshes into Lake St. Clair, emptying into the lake near the entrance of Mitchell's Bay, on the Canada shore.

As I paddled up the shore toward the point where the "Sni Carty" branches off from the main river, I saw a squaw ambling along with a pail in each hand. "Here's milk," quoth I.

I swung the canoe in and said in the most insinuating tones:

"Good morning, ma'am!"

No answer; she kept right on.

"Hello, I want some milk!"

Not a sign of recognition.

"Will you sell me some milk?" I persisted as the canoe kept along with her.

She stopped suddenly and faced me, and set down the pails. She was attired in a Hudson Bay overcoat and an old pair of pantaloons. Oh, dear! how she did lecture me in Chippewa. I gathered from her gestures that she wanted to pull my hair. Things looked squaw'lly. The poor thing evidently thought I was criticising the fit of her ulster. I carefully put a couple of rods of clear, solid water between us. She was hostile, no doubt of it. I sadly left her, and she is talking there yet for all I know.

There are enough Indians on Walpole Island to furnish material for warfare in a first-class blood-and-thunder dime novel. But the noble Lo on Walpole doesn't don warpaint and seek the scalp of the white man. He loafs around and smokes, while his squaw makes baskets to sell, and the lucre is used to procure "fire-water." It is seldom squandered for flour when there is no "fire-water" in the house. These Indians are sufficiently numerous to make, if so disposed, trouble for the Canadian government; but they are used fairly, are peaceable, loyal, and reasonably industrious—for Indians.

I paddled all the morning on the "Sni," along the lovely wooded banks of Walpole. As the day waned the "Ulysses" entered the marshes, through which the channel ran for many miles. It is uniform in width throughout, with water clear as crystal, and fully twenty feet in depth. The margin of the channel is monotonously lined with the tall serges which grow so luxuriantly. Only they who have been in those lonely channels can fully appreciate the square miles of wastes which fill the northern part of Lake St. Clair. My little canoe sat so low on the water that it was impossible to see over the tall grasses that lined the way. There was nothing to contemplate but a desolate line of high weeds to the right and left, and the blue sky over head.

The little canoe and its lonely occupant proceeded farther and farther into the marshes from civilization, and many an ineffectual attempt was made to find a place to land in order to prepare dinner.

It was a splendid locality for fishing, and I put out a trolling line, fastening it to my arm. Three fine bass were soon landed. Suddenly, as I was moving on, a tremendous jerk made me think that I had caught on a log. Before I had recovered from my astonishment it revealed itself a fish. In that lonely place that fish, or whale, or submarine monster, and I had a desperate fight. Two or three times it nearly capsized the canoe; the "Ulysses" was hauled from one side of the channel to the other with railroad speed, until my arms ached. At last another yank, and a lurch, that made my hair rise, the line hauled in light; the spoon hook was gone! I had lost him! I have wished ever since that some well developed steam yacht would seek that place, bait their anchor, and catch that fellow, they will know him; he has my spoon hook.

The sun began to sink toward the west. The "Ulysses" was pointed toward the center of the lake. I had not been able to get dinner, and received a severe cut in attempting to open a box of sardines with a pocket knife. Recollections of stories of storms, accidents and perilous adventures in these marshes came up. After persistent paddling, late in the afternoon voices were heard ahead around a turn in the channel. It was a welcome sound. Six sturdy fellows on a floating derrick, with a huge log half out of the water, indicating that they were clearing the channel, came into view. I came on them suddenly. "What is that smash, dashed thing a comin'?" said the first one that saw me. As if pulled by the same string the six pair of eyes and six mouths opened at me in wonder. Sending the canoe alongside in good style, in less than three minutes the contents of my flask had been divided and put where it would do the most good, and we were acquainted.

They showed me a short cut through the marsh into Mitchell's Bay. A favoring breeze sprung up and by sundown I had made the little French settlement on the shore of the Canadian Lake St. Clair, several miles away from the Chenel Ecarte, at the point indicated on the map, and snugly ensconced in the humble hostelry yclept the "Hunters' Home," and was taking a gossipy smoke with "mine host."

AN EARLY CANOE TRIP.

CHAPTER II.

> "How easy 'tis when destiny proves kind,
> With full spread sails to run before the wind!
> But those that 'gainst stiff gales laveering go
> Must be at once resolved and skilful too."
> —*Dryden.*

A NIGHT AT HUNTERS' HOME—IN A STORM OUT IN THE LAKE—
AN EPISODE WITH A DOG—SKIRTING THE SHORES
OF LAKE ST. CLAIR.

I engaged a Frenchman—a little, old, dried up man—on landing to help carry the canoe to the tavern. As we were about to pass his cabin on the road his wife sallied out, armed with a club—as Col. Sellers would say, a well developed splinter of wood. She placed herself in the middle of the road and showed decided signs of war. The little man at the other end of the canoe trembled. Her club was long enough to defend the road, which had on either side a ditch of water. She was talking in the Canadian French patois with great vehemence, and at intervals would swing her bludgeon with awe-inspiring dexterity.

When we approached to within a respectful distance she shouted in the dialect of the region, which the reader will remember has no literature: "Arrete donc, gascon! Tu menes pas mon gars a l'auberge. Mon beau bijou tiens il se endra jamais au saloon!"

An attempt at remonstrance met with rebuff.

"Avance donc, caribou! Passe le pichou! Sacre gi, tu me passeras pas avec ton canoe d'inde!" she yelled, putting the end of her club under my nose. All of which meant that an attempt to pass would be fatal unless her husband was left behind, as I ascertained afterwards.

"Look here!" said I, "we wish to go up this road to the tavern; if you don't let us pass either one side or the other, by the American eagle, we must march right through you."

Her only response was a whish of the club within an inch of my head. She followed up her charge by the war-cry. "Fou ton comp, sacrable creve faim de Boston! La fier crass-s-s-se!!"

Making signs to my affrighted companion that we were to make a rush, at which he turned pale, but assented, and giving a war hoop, we started. But madame, with her terrible club flying, headed us off. We tried to pass to the right, and then made a rush to the left and nearly had my skull cracked for my pains. Finally, in desperation, I started for the ditch. At this conjuncture my fellow sufferer became demoralized, dropped his end of the canoe and fled. Staggering under the canoe, I went splashing into the ditch. As soon as the mud and water could be removed from my eyes I saw the virago chasing him down the road at the rate of "around the world in eighty days." Crawling out from under the canoe a small boy explained matters: "Ze hole man get drunk when go to ze taavern, and ze old woman she won't let heem go."

"Why didn't she say so?" I growled.

"Eh bien," said the boy, "She deed tell you fife, seex taimes!"

From the onlookers, who had by this time collected, I took pains to enlist an unmarried man to help transport my canoe and traps to the tavern.

The evening was mail night, the mail coming once a week to the little out-of-the-way place. Mine host was also the postmaster, and the combined general store, hotel and postoffice was full of the neighboring population, for the most part hardy wood choppers and teamsters. In subdued tones and with sly and scrutinizing glances a good deal was said about the *grande entrez* of the canoeist into the place. The purport of their private conversation could not but be comprehended by the way they grinned; when one of them caught my eye his face would suddenly drop like one caught laughing in prayer meeting by the parson.

Finally, mine host—a Yankee by the way—picked up a bundle of letters and commenced calling for the owners. He gratified himself so far as to read the postal cards, and favored the company with comments on the contents. This is the way he went on: "Ange Cromieaux, come here and get this letter from your girl." The blushing Ange took his letter amid the guffaws of the crowd.

"Pierre Boissant! Ah, ha! old Pierre, one more from the same female." The crowd, regarding this as fine fun, roared. Pierre made an answer in patois that turned the laugh on the postmaster, who rejoined by advising him to get his bald head frescoed before committing matrimony.

"Alex Ledoux, brace up; bad news; your uncle's lost a cow." Another round of laughter. "Thomas Sangtien, your mother-in-law's coming."

These sallies of the postmaster were received with good humor; often with not inappropriate answers in patois. Before getting to the end, he suddenly paused, poised his specs on the end of his nose, and gazed long and anxiously at a postal card.

"Boys," said he, "poor Henri is dead. He died among strangers; here is his last writin', and he died in writin' it, as a stranger has added here. It's to his wife." "Now," he continued, taking off his specs and wiping them, "none

PEN AND INK SKETCH OF MINE HOST.

of us are rich; it's a struggle to get enough to feed and clothe the little ones. Poor Henri was generous and helped when you were in need. There's a new widow in the little cabin over yonder and nine fatherless children. The guardian angel only knows what's to become of them during the long winter a comin'."

Here the postmaster drew the till out from under the counter and turned it bottom up. The coins within gave a muffled jingle.

"Here's what I have taken in and it's for the widow. Who adds to it?"

Several of those present walked up and emptied their pockets, others made pledges. In turn, the stranger approached and added to the little pile, and the postmaster reached his hand over the counter and said:

"Stranger, shake!"

A noted authority on the subject has said: "Every true canoeist will sleep in his canoe." That had been the programme of the writer on starting. Finding upon trial that the shore could be approached, owing to shoals, only in one place, and that place unfit for a camp, for the first and last time during the cruise I slept in a bed, and it was a good one. I was awakened early in the morning by hearing three cheers. Looking out of the window a noble army of geese were seen, confronted by the postmaster, who was holding in his hand a dish of feed. It reminded me forcibly of a ward political meeting.

It was a bright, sunny morning that I parted from my new-made friends. The breeze was fresh, though not favorable, and some sombre-looking clouds reared their heads in the west. The weather was a cause of anxiety, as the cruise, most of the day, would be outside a narrow line of marsh, about two miles from shore, known as Tic-Tac Point, which extended far into the lake and bended down like a hook along the eastern shore.

It is safe to say, within a decade of centuries—and geologists rattle off these periods of time as an auctioneer does a five cent raise on a twenty cent towel—Lake St. Clair will be mostly solid land. A commencement is being made in the immense marshes at the mouth of the River St. Clair. The eastern shore of the lake is now one vast marsh. Ground must have been recovered in this way from the lake, and portions of the peninsulas of Michigan and Canada were once no doubt under water. Tic-Tac Point is a geological inroad upon the lake. A settler thereby informed me from a scow: "There isn't a da-cint place of solid land for a da-cint man to put his fut on."

CAUGHT IN A STORM.

When answered "that if such was the case, I would not make a da-scent upon it," he looked tediously unhappy.

Tic-Tac Point, obliging all crafts to keep well out to sea, will long be remembered. The ominous looking clouds in the west, observed on starting, came up and monopolized nearly the whole sky, and the opposing breeze freshened into a gale. The effect of it was apparent as soon as the "Ulysses" rounded the Point. Great waves lifted the canoe up in the air, rolled under it and buried themselves with an ominous swish among the drift-wood floating in the tall grasses of the marsh near by. It was necessary to paddle toward the open lake to keep out of the trough of the sea. After paddling vigorously for an hour the gale had freshened considerably, and the tops of the waves began to break off into "white caps." Crawling forward in the canoe on hands and knees, the rubber apron and rubber coat were secured from the forward storage compartment, and buttoning the apron over the cockpit, the crew of the storm-tossed craft was soon in waterproof shape. Thanks to the sealed air chambers in either end of the canoe, the gallant little boat rode lightly on every wave. Occasionally a dash of water came over and rolled harmlessly off the apron and deck. Another hour of tedious work with the paddle and such headway had been made as to be out of sight of land, or rather of the marshes.

If paddling was discontinued one moment the canoe came about at once and sank into the trough. There was nothing to do but to stick to it. The compass showed the canoe headed straight to the center of the lake, and after a long and continuous pull at the paddle, which seemed a day, to my intense relief, the wind changed to the northwest. With some difficult work on my hands and knees, I succeeded in stepping the mast, hoisting the little sail, close reefed, and in a moment was booming along to the southeast.

At two o'clock the "Ulysses" had reached the lonely light-house among the marshes at the mouth of the River Thames. Ensconcing the canoe snugly behind a great log in a sheltered nook, I started for the light-keeper's house. As an Irishman once said, "the first person I met was a big dog," who showed a disposition to dine on me, so that it became necessary to unjoint the paddle and carry half of it along to convince him that he musn't, but the dog came for me so vigorously that I was literally obliged to climb an upright timber supporting a range light, and it was accomplished with an agility that would have reflected credit on an organ-grinder's monkey.

"The dearest spot on earth to me,
 Is home, sweet home."
                        —*Old Song.*

I would have soon slipped back into the teeth of the animal, if a little four-year old fellow had not come up and called him off.

One disposed to moralize can easily see how truly great every one is in his own sphere, no matter how humble it is. Here an infant subdues an animal that threatens a man. Fancy what work would Hon. Roscoe Conkling make at scissors grinding! How well would Benjamin F. Butler and Samuel J. Tilden satisfy a crowd of newsboys and boot-blacks with a double-shuffle jig! Imagine Hon. David Davis as a tight rope walker, and, if you will, that good man, President Hayes, selling squirt guns in a public square, or Robert G. Ingersoll as a missionary to the heathen.

The dog quieted, I approached the dwelling of the light keeper. A young girl answered my summons at its door, and informed me that her father was ill. Judging by the look of her face when she saw me, she was divided in the opinion as to whether the stranger before her was a minion of his Satanic Majesty, or an insurance agent in disguise. When I finished a quart pitcher of milk she kindly offered, and which she assured me could be spared, as they "always gave it to the pigs," she gazed at me with open eyes and naively remarked: "You must be *fond* of milk."

After making, in addition, a hearty meal of coffee, cold

meat and crackers at the canoe, when ready to embark again the wind had gone down. In another hour the "Ulysses" had ceased to skirt along marshes, and solid land appeared, the first encountered since leaving Walpole Island. Farewell to the marshes was bidden with pleasure. Late in the afternoon the point where the Great Western Railway first touches the shore of Lake St. Clair, which it runs along for miles was reached. As the trains passed and repassed, the passengers hurried to the windows to get a look at the "Ulysses" and its occupant, which must have appeared a strange object to them.

The storm being passed, the sun reappeared, and just as it sank down in the lake a little settlement came into view. Paddling on to a large tumble-down looking structure with smoke pouring out of the chimney, near the shore, the canoe was beached, and I made the acquaintance of a couple of honest colored men. After preparing supper, I retired to the recesses of the comfortable little canoe, thoroughly wearied with the day's efforts, and, as Shakspeare says:

> "Weariness
> Can snore upon the flint when restive sloth
> Finds the down pillow hard."

CHAPTER III.

> —"Humble voyagers are we,
> O'er life's dim, unsounded sea,
> Seeking only some calm clime,
> Touch us gently, gentle time!"
> —*Barry Cornwall.*

AT A SETTLEMENT—CURIOSITY—THE SUNDAY REST—A STORM ON THE LAKE—JOHNSON'S HYMN.

It was on a Saturday night that the "Ulysses" and its solitary captain reached the little settlement on the shore of, and about half way down, Lake St. Clair.

The settlement on the eastern shore has some importance as being the stopping place of transient trains on the Great Western Railway of Canada. The sudden advent of a queer looking stranger apparently from nowhere, unless from out of the lake, was a surprise to two colored men who lorded it over the beach as workmen, in an old tumble-down building used as a pearl ashery. The inhabitants in the vicinity made "salts" by boiling wood ashes into a powerful black lye which they sold to the ashery. A process of boiling and roasting converted the lye into beautiful white pearlash. It is then shipped to England and returned to this country as saleratus, where it not only raises biscuit, but, according to dentists, raises the dickens with the teeth. An example of the strength of the product was made, as the colored man, who luxuriated under the cognomen of Johnson, the presiding genius of the place, was explaining the process. A couple of settlers, Frenchmen, drove up with a load of the "salts." It was contained in large wooden troughs. They had not completed unloading when I was surprised to see both lift their hands in the air, utter wild yells and rush to the lake, where they plunged their arms in the water up to their elbows. They had accidently spilled "salts" on their hands. Mr. Johnson said unless speedily washed off, "de stuff would eat froo to de bone."

The arrival of the "Ulysses" was soon talked about, and the people came to view it and be inquisitive.

"What is it made of?" "What did it cost?" are the questions the canoeist must answer until he feels like hoisting a placard at the bow containing, in big type, the desired information.

The "Ulysses" was built of wood one-eighth of an inch thick, consisting of three pieces of thin veneer glued crosswise and afterwards pressed into boat shape. The veneer makes a combination very stiff and strong, and

THE TWO ORPHANS.

"Be you travelin' in that thing?"

finished in the natural grain of the wood. It presents a beautiful appearance, and to the eye looks as if made of a single piece. This appearance causes the owner of this kind of a canoe to do a world of explaining.

The interlocutor looks at you as if he would have been a great deal happier if you had lied to him about the cost. I was so strongly convinced of this as to make up my mind to try the effect of a mild yarn on a stranger when a good chance offered. It came at the Pearlash settlement.

The "Ulysses" was approached by "two orphans," *i. e.* a tall, seedy looking man, and a lean, seedy looking dog. The man pointed his nose at the canoe and asked:

"Be you a travelin' in that?"

"I am."

"Been far?"

"I have."

"Goin' far?"

"I am, sir."

"What are you doin' it for?"

"Fun."

"Whew-w-" said the man, who looked at me as if I was a choice specimen. "What did it cost?'

"Five hundred and eighty dollars."

He puckered his mouth to the size of a safe key and

remarked: "It's expensive to be sure, but it's a good thing to have in the family, young man. You can use the blamed thing for a coffin some day." Another day at Detroit a delapidated looking youngster shouted from the wharf: "Say, cap'n, wot did that 'ere boat cost?" His inquiry was answered. "Well," he replied "you ken just send me up a half a dozen." The cost is a question of moment, and more people are interested in it than he that pays it.

After supper that night I walked half a mile from the shore, and went to the post-office and general store. As usual, it was full of settlers—on boxes, on barrels, on the counter, and even on the stove. The stranger received the best chair, and was then and there sailed into, so to speak, and questioned until the tobacco smoke which obscured the room, seemed to twist every inmate into an interrogation point. I finally retreated in a blaze of glory, after having shown them how a light hammock hat I wore could be taken off, folded up, and put into a vest pocket. Passing out one of them was heard to remark: "That feller is all j'ints; he unj'ints his paddle, his mast and his boom, pockets his hat, unscrews his legs, and packs himself in that blasted canoe. He's built in sections, sure."

That night camp was made in a rather lonely spot on

SAY, CAP'N, WOT DID THAT ERE BOAT COST?

the shore, near a piece of woods. About two o'clock a howl, as if from some beast truly infernal, started me out of a sound sleep. Peering over the edge of the canoe did not enable me to distinguish anything in the darkness. Finally, when the muffled tread in the sand paused beside my canoe and it stood fairly over me, I jumped up in affright and confronted a donkey. If my recollection serves, I adjured him in the noble language which Shakespeare puts in the mouth of the conscience stricken Macbeth on seeing Banquo's ghost, and he kindly left.

The next day, Sunday, the day of rest, dawned beautifully. After a bath in the lake an exploration of the country was in order. During the stroll a young girl was encountered carrying pails of milk. She had on an immense straw hat nearly as large as an umbrella. Taking out my note book and commencing to sketch her appearance as she approached, and the hat covering her eyes, she never discovered me until she had almost reached me. Her gaze was caught first by my fancy slippers, and wandered furtively up to the note book and pencil; then she gave a scared look into my face, taking in the red fez and exclaiming "Mon Dieu!" she fled.

The big hat flopped up and down like a distressed balloon, and the milk splashed out of the pails along the mud road, making a veritable "milky way."

There was to be a picnic in the afternoon for the benefit of the church, including as attractions beer and dancing. I took note of the bonnets of the ladies, and also of their owners, from a point of vantage on the steps of the store, watching the vehicles drive past to the rendevouz. It was a happy crowd, and though there was a diversity in style of the headgear of the ladies—bless 'em—they were apparently as happy as if the great Worth, of Paris, had built the things, and charged them a hundred dollars or so apiece for the bits of filagree.

Later in the afternoon a fine beam wind sprung up. The opportunity was not to be lost, as time was precious. So the canoe was launched, the sail was hoisted, and the "Ulysses" was shortly speeding away toward the Detroit River. At the end of an hour the wind shifted, and clouds began to pile up in the direction in which the canoe was headed. Passing a wood scow anchored off the shore, the skipper shouted:

"You'd better get on land with that pumpkin seed!"

I began to think it good advice, and given none too soon. A few drops of rain pattered on the deck, and the wind freshened. The canoe was on the lee shore of the lake, and

the long breakers began to roll in, making it hard work to paddle, so deeming it hazardous to go on, I put about, only accomplishing it after much hard effort and no little peril. While doing this the breakers began to roll in, larger and faster. I nervously watched their approach as I had the canoe partially turned, and was wallowing in the trough. The gallant little "Ulysses" shot up on every crest buoyant as a feather, and the breakers went roaring and tearing at the shore in the distance. Finally getting about, and giving the little sail, close-reefed, to the now favoring gale, the canoe bounded over the rollers towards my recent camping ground, which was soon reached, much to the relief of my honest colored friend, Johnson, of the ashery. "Chile, I knewed ye was bobbin' 'roun' out dar like an egg in a pail. I felt powerful anxious. When yo' get to yo' home, jes yo' stay thar. Keep away from de lee shoah, speshally ob dis yere lake. You're bound to get berry, berry damp some of dese days, shuah."

I had hardly been ensconced in a snug corner of the ashery before a blazing log fire, when "the winds blew and the rain descended" most terrifically.

My friend Johnson entertained me for a long time with original discourses upon moral and religious subjects.

He finally became reflective, and fell to sermonizing. "A

man's jes' like an ole wheel. Dar's de tire. Dat's his outah coverin'. Dar's de felloes. Dar's de spokes—de frame. Las'ly, dar's de hub. Dat's his h'art. What's a wheel good for wid a rotten hub un'm, eh? or a man?" I surrendered to Mr. Johnson.

The afternoon darkened into night, and the wind blew furiously outside, tearing at the loose boards on the old building, while the breakers kept roaring on the beach. Johnson and his assistant were engaged in singing negro melodies. Sitting in front of the blazing logs, one of these hymns attracted notice as being particularly striking The following is a verse:

> " Some day you'll be a knockin' at de gate;
> I'm agoin' to go froo dar if I kin;
> Ole Peter he will meet yo' an' tell your fate;
> I'm agoin' to go froo dar if I kin.
> When Gabrell comes an' blows de las' trump;
> I'm agoin' to go froo dar if I kin.
> If yo' want to get in you'll jes have to jump;
> I'm agoin' to go froo dar if I kin.

IN PERIL.

CHAPTER IV.

> But oars alone can ne'er prevail
> To reach the distant coast,
> The breath of heaven must swell the sail,
> Or all the toil is lost."
> —*Cowper.*

PLEASURES OF CANOEING—ON A ROCK—SINGULAR RIVERS—A GHASTLY CARGO—THE DETROIT RIVER—A HORRIBLE DISCOVERY.

A cruising canoe will hold but one person, who must cruise alone or secure the company of a congenial friend. If anything will bring out the innate badness in human nature it is a journey in company. It is a rare friendship at best that will stand the test. Then there is a great deal of enjoyment to be had in a canoe alone. Many people have said to the writer:

"Canoeing would be delightful, except for the journeying alone.

That is a mistake. A canoeist is the most independent being imaginable, and as he carries with him his house, his bed and his board, the ordinary conditions of life do not circumscribe him, and he is purely and utterly free. This sense of freedom is glorious. The grand panorama of nature that in infinite variety delights his eye; the incident of travel, to which adventure lends a spice, combine to make a canoeing experience so charming that it is sure to be repeated.

A hard gale had prevailed all day, confining me to my camp. The next day found the gale still raging, but from a more favorable quarter for sailing. Time was precious and a start must be made. All the male population of the little settlement turned out to see the "Ulysses" and its captain depart.

The lee shore of a shallow lake, with a gale sweeping its whole twenty miles of width, is not an attractive cruising ground for a boat only thirteen feet long and with only one eighth of an inch of wood between its crew and the bottom; but the capabilities of the little canoe were so well known that it was with no feeling of danger I embarked, in spite of the warning of friends on shore.

The government charts showed dangerous shallows and boulders off Stony Point, and to avoid these it was necessary to make a detour in the open lake, and with sail up the "Ulysses" bounded lightly over the waves toward Detroit. The combined action of a quartering sea and a beam wind forced the canoe to the leeward. Drifting towards shore, unperceived by me, suddenly I was startled

LADIES AND GENTLEMEN'S STYLES.—*Page 64.*

1. "Neat Straw." 2. "Latest Agony." 3. "Heavy." 4. "Stylish."
5. "Chic."

by a violent shock. The canoe had run upon a submerged boulder. Then a roller lifted the canoe up in the air and receding let it come down with a thud, causing it to heel over dangerously. Another heavy swell followed, and, before the sail could be lowered, three times the canoe rose upon the waves and came down with a heavy shock. It shivered like a leaf, and I expected momentarily to feel the water come curling up around me inside. Carefully balancing and reaching under with the paddle when the next wave raised it, a vigorous shove sent the canoe into deep water. Luckily it had struck every time upon its solid oaken keel, and had sustained no injury.

Three or four rivers are marked on the charts as emptying into the lake; but they do not empty, at least not after a protracted eastern gale. The sand from the lake bottom is thrown forward by the waves, making a dam across the mouths of these rivers, shutting them off entirely, and leaving them simply water courses from the lake extending in the form of rivers far back into the country. During the dry season the flow of water from the river is not sufficient to break through the bar of sand at the mouth. It is only in the gentle spring time, and after the fall rains, that they get up enough enthusiasm to flow. Perhaps it is not going too far to say they soon get discouraged. Hence they are quiet streams—so quiet as to be at times quite stagnant. As Artemus Ward would say, near the close confines at the mouths of these so-called rivers is a beautiful country for one's wife's relations to live in.

But withal, the vigorous descendants of the hardy French settlers that dwell in that section live there and thrive, enjoying life to the utmost. We associate malaria with such regions, and if there is anything of the kind bordering that portion of Lake St. Clair, the Frenchmen there take to fever and ague as naturally as a young lady to a new bonnet; and it doesn't seem to hurt them much either. Like the young lady and the bonnet, they miss it if they don't have it.

At four in the afternoon I had reached to where Belle river should be, according to the chart. It was not there. Seeing some men digging on the shore, I asked:

"Where is the mouth of Belle river?"

"Its dammed!" was the extraordinary reply.

"No doubt, but where is it!"

"Here."

"That's the shore."

"Its dammed! I tell you," yelled the man.

Not being able to imagine why the man should swear so singularly at a civil question, I went ashore. The man was

MR. JOHNSON.

"A man 's jes' like an ole wheel."—*Page 58.*

A GHASTLY CARGO.

right—the last gale had sent a drift of sand clear across the mouth of the river and surely enough it was *dammed*, and they were digging the sand away to release a couple of scows.

Making a hasty meal here, the head of the "Ulysses" was again pointed along the shore. The wind by this time had completely died away. Seeing a low, black hulled sail-boat in the distance, lying becalmed, with huge patched sail hanging listlessly, the canoe was directed toward it. On coming near enough it was seen to have a ghastly cargo. Skulls grinned from the deck, and bones protruded in every direction from the gaping mouths of bags, with which the vessel was laden. In the stern sat a red-haired man, smoking. He had picked these bones up along the shore and was taking them to the city to sell.

"When do you expect to reach Detroit?" I asked.

"Bedad, sor! I'm a thinkin' loike it will be the next Cintinnial at the prisint rate of goin'." He was not French!

The Canada shores of Lake St. Clair are strewn with millions of feet of logs, planks and timbers, also with trees, stumps, and here and there the melancholy remains of a vessel. This accumulation of drift is a surprising sight. In the shallows along the shore are many submerged trees and stumps, and it required constant care to prevent impaling the canoe on a snag.

The glorious afternoon mellowed into sunset. The sun went down in roseate splendor, the moon came up and the "Ulysses" was yet far from the Detroit River. Vigorous work at the paddle brought the light on Windmill Point into view, and in an hour the shores of "Isle de la Peche," in the entrance of the river, came into sight.

Passing a scow becalmed, the canoe was directed alongside. I was almost overcome with horror on beholding a human head was hanging over the rail. It was the head of a man; his eyes were closed and the moon shone full in his face.

"Hello!" I shouted.

No answer!

Was he dead?

Reaching up with the paddle I touched the livid face, and was greatly relieved to find it was only the death of drunkenness. Spenser's words might be applied:

> "The messenger approaching him spake,
> But his waste words returned to him in vain
> So sound he slept that naught might him wake."

After sawing the blade of the paddle once or twice up and down under his nose, which only evoked a prolonged snore, I left him to his sweet repose.

It was nine o'clock when the "Ulysses" shot from the Canada channel behind "Isle de la Peche" into the quiet bosom of the Detroit River. The canoe was directed towards the head of Belle Isle. Beyond could be seen the lights of the city. A large Lake Superior propeller loomed up in the distance, her red and green lights visible, and indicating that I was directly in her course.

An overpowering odor saluting my nostrils and perceiving a black object ahead, I approached. The sight the moonlight revealed to me that night made an impression on me that lived in my memory for many a day. It was a dead and floating human body. The eyes were fixed, staring open, and the hair was tossed and matted on the bloated face.

Acting on the impulse, I seized the paddle and was about to leave the vicinity, but reflecting that it was my duty to secure the body and bring it to the city, I set about preparing a rope. Before this could be done, however, I had to paddle vigorously to get out of the way of the propeller, which had approached unperceived. As it was, I narrowly escaped being run down. The little canoe danced on the heavy swells, and after the propeller passed I found the body had disappeared. The swell of the steamer had sunk it. As

I paddled away I looked around, as did the "Ancient Mariner" of Coleridge.

> "Like one that on a lonesome road,
> Doth walk in fear and dread;
> And, having once turn'd round, walks on,
> And turns no more his head
> Because he knows a frightful fiend
> Doth close behind him tread."

The canoe was soon in the shadows at the head of Belle Isle and proceeded down the American channel into the region of wharves and shipping; as the great bell in the City Hall was striking eleven, the "Ulysses" had been safely housed and its captain trod once more the streets of the city, said by travelers to be the loveliest in the land.

CHAPTER V.

> "Thus with imagined wings our swift scene flies
> In motion with no less celerity
> Than that of thought."
> —*Shakspeare.*

EN ROUTE TO LAKE ERIE—SCENES ALONG THE DOCKS—A DOSE OF NITRO-GLYCERINE.

Detroit River, from Lake St. Clair to Lake Erie, was the concluding part of the cruise laid out for the "Ulysses." That would complete the journey from Lake Huron to Lake Erie. After a stay of several days in Detroit, where I was again joined by Joe, one sunshiny October afternoon found us on the beautiful Detroit River in the "Halloo" and "Ulysses," headed southwards, towards Lake Erie. The usual crowd of idlers and small boys witnessed our departure, and bombarded us with questions.

As we left, a couple of newsboys were holding a "canoe congress" on the dock. Before we were out of sight we could see that from logical reasoning they had descended to personal argument and were pummelling each other in a truly emphatic way.

We paddled down stream past the docks, the shipping,

among the smoking tugs, carefully avoiding the ferries crossing to Canada. The swells of the huge steamer Great Western made our little craft bob about like corks.

Just below the elevator we were joined by a man in a row-boat:

"What are them consarned things?" said he.

"Fellow-pilgrim o'er the watery waste," replied Joe, "I will tell thee. Archæological research develops indubitably the fact that the aboriginal species of the *genus homo* were not only deplorably deficient in information regarding the use of calorics in the preparation of substance with which to replete the alimentary function——"

"I don't tumble," interrupted the man.

"Please don't," said Joe; "you'll get wet. As I was saying, as indicated, ethnologically, by the conformation of the *occiput frontalis*, this species exhibit in all departments of their domestic and physical economy equally denuded understanding, especially so in the *modus operandi* of conveyance along aqueous surroundings. See?"

"Oh, y-y-yes, I see," hesitatingly answered the man, with a dazed look.

"I knew you would," continued Joe, "how adjacent this period of existence was to the post-tertiary, anthropologists are unable to efficiently determine; probably the ethnic

A CANOE CONGRESS.

"That ere boat's made of wood!"
"T'aint nuther!"

epoch marked by the brachycephalic *crania*——" The man began to move off.

"Where are you going?" asked Joe.

"To get out of here," said the man.

"Aren't you a gentleman of culture?" inquired Joe.

"No, by thunder!" yelled the man, "I belong in Windsor; I never was in that place, and I don't want to be;" and he made the water foam behind his oars as he rowed away.

Paddling along the crowded docks of a large city is quite different from cruising in a wilderness. Every man at work on vessels or on the wharf that observed us, felt impelled to stop work and yell at the canoeists.

They told us to part our hair in the middle. We were invited to give information as to our canoes, and one wanted to engage a cabin passage. In short, we could have started a semi-naval land engagement several times, had we been so disposed. Away down the river, snugly ensconced behind a lumber pile on the dock, we came upon a man taking an astronomical observation. He had a long black bottle elevated toward the sky at an angle of forty-five degrees. His lips imbibed the orifice, and we could see

"The swallows homeward fly."

We approached him without his hearing us.

"Hello!" we yelled.

"Hello yourself!" said the man, taking down the bottle. "I'd just like to know if a man can't come here to take a little medicine for his cough without being shouted at that way?"

We begged his pardon, and paddled away. He yelled after us: "I'd offer you some, boys, but there's no directions on the label about the dose for 'infants.'"

We proceeded down the river leisurely, past vessels, lumber piles, manufactories, and, finally, Fort Wayne, where the guns of Uncle Samuel frown across the river upon devoted Canada, and where the recreative soldiers fish off the dock; past the officers' quarters among the trees on the high bank, and at last were fairly below the city and its surroundings.

Great flocks of ducks flew over head, and we could occasionally hear the bang of the sportsman's gun in the marshes lining the shore below the River Rouge.

Twice we had a shot with a revolver at a flock resting on the water, once dropping a bullet in among them. It was twilight before the canoes skirted the low shores of Fighting Island, which is occupied by fishermen, whose shanties are built along the river, and which owes its name to the

AN ASTRONOMICAL OBSERVATION.

fact that it has been the scene of many professional pugilistic encounters.

The twilight had deepened when we reached Grassy Island, which being nothing but a shoal with rushes, we paddled right through it. A boy rowed out to us from the light-house near by, and began to ask the usual questions. Joe called him confidentially up to his canoe, and told the youth something that made him stare at me in a frightened manner. He said I had accidently swallowed a pint of nitro-glycerine, and that he was a committee of one appointed to escort me out of town, as it was feared I would explode; for that reason I was not allowed to ride on the cars and must travel by water. Joe solemnly cautioned the boy not to say anything to make me laugh, as I would "burst—sure." The boy didn't.

Soon after we arrived at Wyandotte, and paddling under the cloud of smoke from the iron works that hung over the river, soon reached the head of Grosse Isle. The surface of the water was like a mirror, and the stars, reflected from the sky above, twinkled around us in the water like dots of fire. It was after seven o'clock when our canoes were hauled into the boat house at the summer residence of a friend on the island, a prince among good fellows.

The next morning early we were again on the river, and

in a driving rain paddled down the romantic wooded shores of the island.

By ten o'clock we had reached the Lime-Kiln Crossing. A thick mist had now settled about us; the rain came down harder and drove in our faces; we were keeping close together; suddenly our canoes brought up with a terrific bump against some floating object, and a man came out upon it, yelling madly at us, "There's nitro-glycerine on this float; get away from here, quick! You'll be blowed up!"

Joe responded: "I'm a married man and I'm used to it," but paddled away for dear life. We had run into the government drilling scow engaged in blasting the rocks on the reef.

A few moments later we were cruising along the shores of Sugar Island, in the mouth of the river, and at the end of half an hour our canoes were dancing on the broad bosom of Lake Erie. Hailing a passing tug, bound up, we were taken aboard, with our canoes, and were soon proceeding up the river.

FACES FROM THE DOCKS.

CHAPTER VI.

> "I've watched and travelled hard;
> Sometime I shall sleep out; the rest I'll whistle."
> —*Shakspeare.*

A JOLLY TUG CAP'N—A SPEECH FROM JOE—A LOST COW—ROMEO AND JULIET—HOME—DELIGHTS AND REVERSES OF CANOEING.

The hale, hearty old captain of the tug on which we had embarked with our canoes, with a contempt for small craft, that always lingers in the bosom of men of his class, dubbed our boats "Lunatic Asylums." "To be sure," he added, "they won't hold but one; but there's room for a plaguey big one."

Joe told him that we were agents "employed to distribute tracts on swearing to tug captains."

The old man, laughing, replied: "Well, now! you *can* tell, for sure, the difference between a tug cap'n and a parson by jest a hearin 'em talk a leetle, especially if the tug cap'n's riled. That reminds me of old cap'n Bob Stivers. Now, that man couldn't no more help swearing than a pirate; why, one time he let his vessel go on the rocks—

took so much time to swear he didn't give his orders in quick enough. One time his wife's sister, a conscientious sort of a critter, started home from the theater with him—told him she wouldn't go a step with him if he swore. Bob held out first-rate until they got part way home, and then let out an old double-decker. She stopped. He had jest pursuaded her to start when he did it agin. Got her started agin, and swore some more, and so on over and over. Will you believe me, it took that poor man until two o'clock in the morning to go half a mile with her—fact!"

A short ride with this jolly mariner brought us to Amherstburg, a small town on the Canada side, near the mouth of the river—the first port after leaving the lake. We could have proceeded to Detroit on the tug, but had made the resolution to make the round trip in our canoes; so we unloaded them on the dock amid a miscellaneous crowd of onlookers, collected in spite of the pouring rain.

Joe muttered to me: "Now's a chance; see how long they will stay, and not a soul has an umbrella." Mounting a pile of lumber, with the rain dripping from his rubber coat, he commenced:

"*Fellow citizens:* I am proud to appear here before you on this auspicious occasion; and I may add that I am proud to have this glorious opportunity to raise my voice in a place which, I am credibly informed, is the center of culture, civilization and philosophic thought for this adjacent vicinity, if not more so; and as I stand here and a realization of the grandeur of my paramount mission reminds me of duty it repels burning words which crowd upon my lips for utterance—

Here a small boy in the crowd yelled to a distant small boy—

"Johnny, come here and hear the preachin'," and a big man swore, shook the rain off his hat and ran for shelter.

"I am here on a most important errand, and what is that errand?" continued Joe. "Will you stand here

> "Dumb as statues,
> Or unbreathing stones,"

and not aid me? Will this enlightened community be aware, and not assist? Will you—

"What's the errand?" shouted an impatient squint-eyed man, with a drop of rain trickling down his nose.

"Brother Jones," said Joe, turning to me, "will you prepare to take up a collection?"

Here the squint-eyed man and two-thirds of the crowd incontinently left.

"On the gulf of Leaotong, China," resumed Joe, "lies the town of Neuchwang, and—

Here I made a motion as if to pass the hat, and all the rest hastily left, except a small boy, who said to Joe, as he got down off the lumber—

"Look a here, parson, you've struck the wrong crowd for collections."

We made our way to the hotel and waited for fair weather, which did not come until the next morning, then with a good up river breeze. We launched our canoes off the dock, and shortly were having a grand fight with the heavy current prevailing at the railroad ferry crossing of the Canada Southern Railway. It was a question for a time which conquered—wind or water—and, as is often the case in affairs on this mundane sphere, wind prevailed, and our little craft, under the influence of the fresh breeze, were soon skirting along the high banks of Grosse Ile crowned with summer residences.

Just below where the ruins of a fire-stricken hotel are marked by a desolate black spot in a green sward and a lonely pier extending into the river, we were hailed by a man from the shore.

"Have you seen a cow?" he asked.

"Have you lost one?" responded Joe.

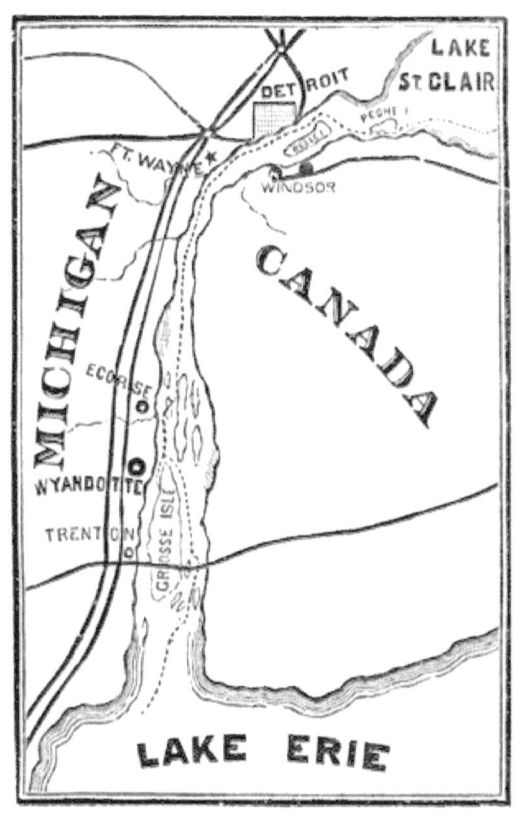

MAP OF DETROIT RIVER.

"Yes!"

"Is she of the *genus amphibii?*"

"I dunno," replied the man, puzzled.

"Was she web footed?" asked Joe.

"Pshaw, no!"

"We haven't seen your cow then," answered Joe, sadly. "My friend you do not know that you awakened a wild longing hope in my breast only to dash it to atoms. I am sorry we haven't seen your cow. Now if we had sailed up on the shore we might have met a land cow; but I fondly, wildly hoped when you first spoke, there might be an aquatic cow; that I could give the fact to the world and go down to my grave honored as the man who had solved the problem of ages as to how so much water gets into boarding house milk."

The man gave Joe an appealing look, and with all his might scrambled up the bank without looking back.

An hour later we were snugly ensconced in the dining room of the summer home of our friend of the voyage down, and after a hearty dinner were once more *en route* for Detroit, sailing up the Canada side of the river.

Off the Sulphur Springs, below Sandwich, Canada, the "Ulysses" narrowly escaped being wrecked; the sail partially hid the course of the canoe ahead, and as it was dashing along under the influence of a puff of wind, there suddenly loomed into view a clump of huge spiles only five feet away. The canoe was headed directly for them and it seemed almost an impossibility to avoid a collision. The rudder was veered to the port side with an energy born of despair, and I held my breath as the end of the boom just grazed them.

An hour later we had entered the region of tugs, ferries and shipping. We maintained our cruise along the docks on the Canadian shore, at one place nearly being deluged by a bucket of slops thrown over the side of a vessel. Joe being nearest the point of danger gave vent to his feelings by giving a blood curdling yell, the immediate effect of which was to bring into sight over the rail of the vessel, two piggy eyes, a red nose and a wide mouth, the property of the female cook.

"Oh, Juliet!" exclaimed Joe, bringing his canoe into the wind and standing up he apostrophized her:

> "Oh! speak again, bright angel! for thou art
> As glorious to this night, being o'er my head,
> As a winged messenger of heaven
> Unto the white upturned wondering eyes
> Of mortals that fall back to gaze on him,
> When he bestrides the lazy pacing clouds,
> And sails upon the bosom of the air."

AN AQUATIC COW.

The owner of the eyes, the nose and the mouth disappeared a moment and reappeared with a stick of wood elevated to throw.

"Move on, sonny," she said, and Joe moved.

In a little while our canoes were dodging among the ferries and the tugs at Detroit, and at the end of another half hour the "Halloo" and "Ulysses" were safely housed. The voyage was over. The cruise was finished.

This ended the cruise of the "Ulysses," from Lake Huron, around the shore of Lake St. Clair, and through the Detroit to Lake Erie, and surveying the incidents and adventures of the cruise now, the writer cannot but conclude that canoeing is a rare combination of pleasure and incident.

The varied beauties of nature that are unfolded before the gaze of the *voyageur;* the sensation of being soaked through by an untimely rain; the impressiveness of forests musical with the twitterings of birds and made brilliant by patches of golden sunshine; the doubtful happiness of getting stuck in the mud; the pleasure of lying face-upward at night in the canoe—home by water and land—when the wanderer sees the starry host of heaven

"Rising
Through the mellow shade,
Glitter like a swarm of fire-flies tangled in a silver band."

the gyrations of the festive mosquito around a sleepless nose; the unmoved water reflecting the landscape and delighting the eye to the fullest; the anguish connected with a melted coffee pot; the glorious exercise in open air, and ravenous appetites; the terpsichorean efforts resulting from burned fingers at the camp fire; the excitement of adventure and the sad, terrible, lost feeling, that wrings the very soul of the canoeist, when he discovers he has sweetened his coffee with the salt.

All these things exist in the category of a canoe cruise, but the trials make the manly canoeist more manly, and the pleasures indescribably recreate him.

And to such as have not experienced them, the advice, at least, of one enthusiast, is, buy a canoe and try it, even if at the risk of being called a lunatic by your relations.

CONCLUSION.

I.

SPEED OF A CANOE UNDER PADDLE AND SAIL.

Canoeing has developed into many queer phases in the United States. Some are disposed to regard canoes in the light of exclusively sailing craft, and to that end model and provide them with center boards and other yacht-like paraphernalia. Others are inclined to discard the sail altogether, and navigate entirely by paddling. Still others speak loudly for the oar in cruising. Opinions depend largely, of course, upon the use the owner desires to put his canoe: whether he is to use it for short pleasure cruising on a lake or bay near home, or in an extended tour on unknown waters. In any event, the experience of prominent canoeists is well worth knowing.

Mr. N. H. Bishop, in his excellent works, speaks of the use of the oar as almost a necessity. The famous Macgregor, of "Rob Roy" fame, states that a cruising canoe can be paddled to average nearly four miles an hour, or about forty miles per day of ten hours, exclusive of aid from sail or current; and that "no man with a row boat could keep up with a canoe on strange rivers for a week." We have it on his authority, also, that the "last" twelve-mile race of his canoe club was won, with the tide, in "eighty-five minutes."*

II.

SAFETY OF CANOES.

The word "canoe," according to Webster, is derived from "*canaoa*," in the language of the Carribees. It is commonly associated with the word and fact, "capsize." But the modern "cruising canoe" is very unlike its ancient progenitor, the log, bark or hide canoe, in this respect. The craft of to-day bearing the name have been improved in model so as to even bear sail in stormy weather; will withstand the heaviest sea, and there seems no limit to their endurance in this respect.

A member of an English canoe club has traversed the sea between Scotland and Ireland; the channel between England and France has been crossed two or three times in

* "Rob Roy" on the Jordan, note, p. 28.

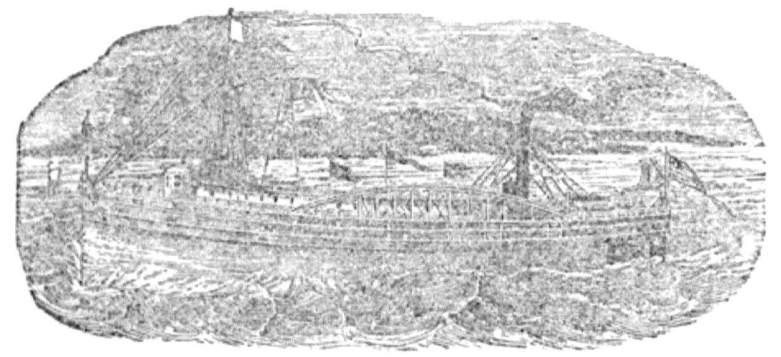

LAKE SUPERIOR PROPELLER.

these tiny craft. A brave American canoeist has made a trip from the north along the Atlantic coast to Florida, and it would require a volume to record the exploits of Macgregor and others, on rivers, in rapids and on sea. Of the two hundred members of the English club, in cruises over Europe, Asia, Africa, America and Australia, not one has been drowned.

III.

LONELINESS.

A well known writer says of cruising alone: "You do not mar your plans by feeble comparisons; you see, hear and think a great deal more than if a 'pleasant companion' is beside you all day, whose small talk (and your own) must be run dry in a month, and neither of you is *free*. In these solitary expeditions I have never a sensation of loneliness. Hard work, healthy exercise, plain food and plenty of it, early hours, reading at night, and working, moving, noting, drawing, observing and considering all day, one's plans are quietly perfected, and there is no more tedium or solitary dullness than when you read or fish alone, or paint or write in a town—the place one can feel the most lonely in after all."*

* Macgregor.

IV.

COST OF OUTFIT AND CRUISING.

A canoe cruise is a most economical as well as a healthful manner of spending a vacation. A canoe can be procured at an expense of from thirty to one hundred dollars, according to completeness, finish, etc. One costing fifty dollars combines all that may be reasonably required for comfort and convenience. A stock of provisions sufficient for two weeks or more can be obtained for fifteen dollars, and providing the voyager sleeps in his canoe and prepares his own food, shunning houses and settlements, as experienced canoeists invariably do, his expenses, making allowance for many luxuries, will average fifty cents per day, or even less. If he cruises in places where food is obtainable at houses and settlements, his expenses need not average more than one dollar per day. It is decidedly cheaper than remaining at home.

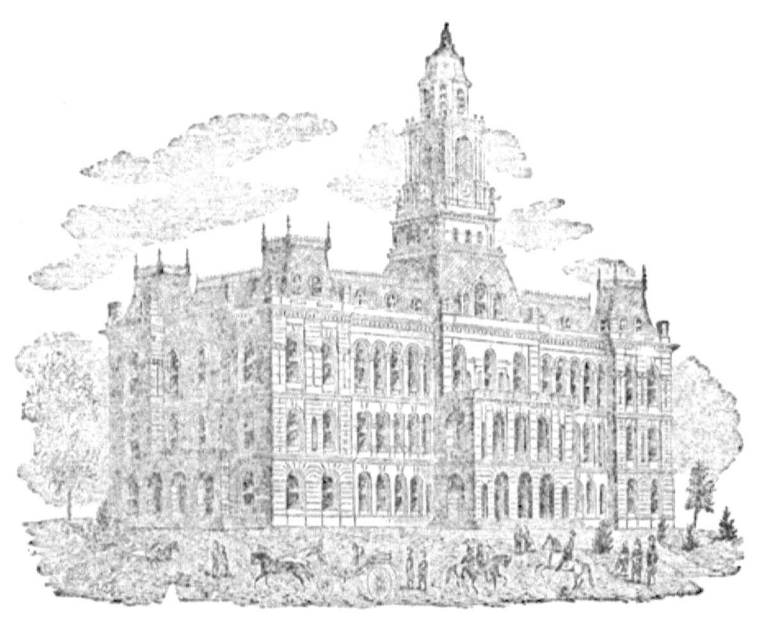

CITY HALL, DETROIT.

www.ingramcontent.com/pod-product-compliance
Lightning Source LLC
Chambersburg PA
CBHW021947160426
43195CB00011B/1249